Live Your Mission

21 Powerful Principles
to Discover Your Life Mission,
After Your Mission

By Andrew Scot Proctor

Table of Contents

Acknowledgements

Ideas are cheap. Execution is priceless. I have been working for years to make this idea into a reality. Many people have helped validate the idea of this book and the book series and a few people have helped me to make it possible.

Special thanks to Christopher Cunningham, the content director at LDS.net and my primary editor for this entire book. My wife, Stacie Proctor, taught me that reaching out to help returned missionaries is an ongoing discussion that isn't limited to one blog post or even one book. This significantly helped me to overcome my fear of a less-than-perfect presentation of this book and every blog post I have published since that conversation. If it weren't for that conversation, this book would not exist. When working on large projects, it makes a world of difference to have a spouse (and best friend) who believes in the highest and best in you.

Other cheerleaders and inspiration for this project have included my parents, my incredible mastermind group friends John Huntinghouse, Alex Barlow, Ben Arkell, Seth Adam Smith, Bekah Pence, Isaac Calvert, Josh Searle, Blake Fischer, Kylee Shields. My religious mentors and teachers Karen Hepworth, Vern Sommerfeldt, Daniel Judd, Brent Topp, Brad Wilcox, Andrew Skinner, S. Kent Brown, Roy Huff and Randy Bott. My inspiring professors who fed the fire of learning in my soul and inspired me to seek truth and to love learning: Stephen Wood, Randall Cluff, James Gough, Jan-Erik Jones, Brent Slife, John Bell, Harold Miller, Robert Ridge and countless others.

I also want to thank those who have made the publication of this book a reality through the Indiegogo campaign: Laurie Pollard, Denis Towers, Dan Buno, Joseph Pearson, Kathleen Cook, Fay Schlather, Amy Johnson, Lisa Weed, Linda Seager, Lauri Hansen,

Mike McConeghey, Dakin Bowman, Dale Bianucci, Sandra Smith, Efhensel, Jane Garner, Melissa Gunn, Brad Partridge, Jan Anderson, Cheryl Lindsay, Michelle Roberts, Tobi Romero, Cary Meyers, Jimmie Westmoreland, Stephanie Clancy, Garin Hess, Abbie Mongie, Todd Galbraith, Joyce Schulz, Christopher Mullen, Kristine Henderson, Linda Beal, Benjamin Bitter, Raven Alard Ngatuvai, David Wilson, Kathy Zarbock, Ekaterina Zharkova, Monica Aranda, Rebekah Miller, Alan Moberly, Terry Jones, Bryant Austin, Ryan Adkins, Chris Evelo, Seblevert, Daniel Dayley, Cindee Nielsen, Adam Allen, Andrew Harward, Laura Jensen, Lynda Spencer, Dallin Duvall, Emilio Nefi, Greg Wurm, John Huntinghouse, Jaimie Francis, María del C., Lara R., Carly Hoffman, Chelsea Grady, Kristin Klein, Dyelan Ballantyne, Brandon Marshall, Nancy Clayson, Lucas Proctor, Kimberly Beckert, Whitney Olsen, Matt Mantyla, Sharon Gurr and R. Dale Jeffery. Some of the contributors have asked not to be included here. My brother Truman Proctor, the sound engineer genius, helped me to figure out how to set up the sound for the audiobook as well and this was immensely helpful!

And an extra special thanks to the amazing photographer Ian Norman, of lonelyspeck.com, who took the photograph used for the cover of this book. Used with permission and under Creative Commons Attribution-ShareAlike 4.0 International.

Introduction

"You will always gravitate toward that which you, secretly, most love."- James Allen

On May 29th, 1975, Steve Prefontaine had just won another five-thousand-meter race at Hayward Field in Eugene, Oregon. This was his 120th win. By this time, he held seven different American records in distance races from the two-thousand to the ten-thousand meters. He ran in the 1972 Olympics representing the United States and was on pace to go to the 1976 Olympics to set a new world record. He was likely the most famous track athlete in the US and possibly the world. No one could stop Pre. He was one of the greatest track legends of all time. Despite his amazing athletic clout, Steve's running career was shattered before he ever reached his full potential as a runner. After a meet celebration at a friends house that night, Steve was driving Frank Shorter, a fellow Olympian, back to where he was staying that night. Just minutes after Steve had dropped off his friend, he was crushed under the weight of his car after it lost control on Skyline Boulevard. One of the most promising athletes to ever live, died at age twenty-four before he had a chance to reach his full potential.

The story of Steve Prefontaine will always haunt me. His whole life seemed to line up for the perfect running career. Steve even predicted his run time to break the world record in the five-thousand meters, which I am fully convinced he would have broken. At his funeral, Bill Bowerman, his coach and the co-founder of Nike, ran the clock for twelve minutes and thirty-six seconds, what Steve predicted as his world-record-breaking time. As if Steve were actually running on the track, four-thousand of his friends, family and fans went wild as the clock ran to a time of 12:36.4, a time that Steve never actually ran.

Steve's story is to me the epitome of incredible human potential that was never reached. Though he was in the perfect position, the five-thousand-meter world record was never broken by Steve Prefontaine. Steve's potential was snuffed out in a moment, but *your* potential is still alive.

That is what this book is about. It's about you reaching your highest potential in this life. There is something that *only you* can contribute to this world. Your unique mission in life. The "five-thousand- meter record" that *only you* can break. It is critical that you discover this because if you don't, your story will be no different than Steve Prefontaine. However, if you discover and live your mission, this world will be a better place because you exist.

Now that you are home from your mission, it may feel like there will never be a more important mission to accomplish than that of a full-time missionary, called by a prophet of God. I used to feel this way, but now I disagree. The most important missionary work you will ever do will be the real-life missionary work as a normal civilian saint. And the best way to be a civilian saint is to discover and live your mission, your life mission. The greatest member missionaries are not the ones who focus their entire efforts and life on finding, teaching and baptizing people. They are the ones who excel in the pathway they have chosen. People like Clayton Christensen, Lindsey Stirling, David Archuleta, Scott Jarvie, Stephanie Nielson, Steven Sharp Nelson, Brandon Flowers and many others. They all excel in their life mission and chosen careers and stand out among the rest, and they also just happen to be members of The Church of Jesus Christ of Latter-day Saints. Their life is their message, and they are authentic, real people. No name tags. Just real people who live the gospel every day and love what they do. You don't need to become famous or be a Mormon celebrity to be this kind of missionary. If you don't believe me, read Clayton Christensen's book *The Power of Everyday Missionaries*. However, I believe you will find even more joy than you ever did on your full-time mission if you live the gospel *while* discovering and living your unique life mission.

2

As a full-time missionary, you know your calling, and you can read your purpose and even memorize it verbatim (it's on page one of *Preach My Gospel*). But when you come home, what is your purpose? What is your calling after the prophetic mission call expires? I believe your purpose now that you are home is to discover your life mission, and to *live your mission*. And until you find that purpose and mission, you may find yourself jumping from one major to another and from one job to another. In the end, as James Allen has said, "You will always gravitate toward that which you secretly, most love." (*As a Man Thinketh*, "Visions and Ideals"). So how do you discover your personal life mission?

This book will provide you with twenty-one powerful principles to help you discover your life mission. Once you do discover it, I will show you how you can *live your mission* every day of your life.

Those who find and live their mission while living the gospel are the greatest missionaries and are ultimately the ones who are happiest in this life. I want to see you break the world record. Don't let your potential be killed before your greatest race. Discover your life mission and live your mission.

Okay, let's get started!

My Unique Life Mission

In some of the chapters in this book, I talk about when I discovered my unique life mission. However, I never say what it is for the purpose of the flow of the chapter. So that you know I'm not a hypocrite as I write this book about discovering and living your mission, here is *my* personal mission in life:

My mission in life is threefold: 1. To be a happy, confident and solid husband and father who is a man of God. 2. To be a powerful voice for good inside and outside of the Church. 3. To inspire good men and women to become *great*—to become their highest selves. To help people remember who they really are and who they always have been. To be a catalyst for all people who are willing, to realize their full potential.

Author's Notes

1. I would LOVE to hear the stories as your read any of these principles in the book. Please visit www.andrewscotproctor.com and find my social media profiles. Tweet me, friend me, email me, find me. I want to hear about it as you go along! I'd love any feedback about any of these principles/chapters as well. I'm used to blogging where it's much easier to comment on a blog post, but please reach out. I want to hear from you, from this book.

2. For the record, this book is my own opinion and should never be understood to represent the doctrine or opinion of The Church of Jesus Christ of Latter-day Saints. I try to stay true to this doctrine, but remember I am a lay member of a lay church, and this is my opinion not doctrine.

Chapter 1

Remember Who You Are,
Not What You Do: Roles VS. Identity

"Today you are you. That is truer than true.
There is no one alive who is youer than you."- Dr. Suess

In April of 2015, I published an article on www.ldsmissionaries.com that got over six hundred thousand organic impressions on our Facebook page. It was an April Fools joke. The title was "Unmarried Returned Missionaries: New Option to Apply for Second Full-time Mission." It posed as a Church announcement to make returned missionaries think that if they hadn't gotten married yet, they had the chance to apply for a second full-time mission. We stopped promoting it after the holiday was over, but it was one of our most popular posts ever. Hundreds of comments poured in from returned missionaries who were angry at the fact that this was a joke. I began receiving emails from hopeful RMs saying that they wished that this was possible. The fact that this article went viral within the LDS niche is an indication to me that there are tens of thousands of returned missionaries who haven't yet figured out their purpose after the mission. I believe a huge reason is because they haven't separated their role from their identity.

When you come home from your mission, you will have to face a big question:

Who am I now?

You have been a missionary for your whole mission. You had a name tag and a prophetic assignment. As a missionary, you are taught to make it a part of you, but being a missionary is a *role* not a characteristic of your identity. Your role has been to be a full-time missionary. Your whole mission you could say "I am a missionary," and it was true.

As you seek to discover and live your unique life mission, you need to understand your identity. Not just the role or roles that you take on, but your identity—the core characteristics of who you are. How can you tell the difference? I'll give you some examples of roles and then some examples of characteristics of identity.

Examples of roles:

- Full-time missionary
- Husband/wife
- Mother/father
- Student
- SEO specialist
- Photographer
- Runner
- Internet entrepreneur
- Sunday School teacher
- Blogger
- Author
- Dancer
- A member of the LDS Church
- Marketer
- Doctor
- CEO
- Elder's Quorum president
- Bilingual

You could add the words "I'm a . . . " before each of the *roles* but not one of these roles could truly describe who you really are deep down. Though you have been a full-time missionary your whole mission, saying "I'm a missionary" does not describe who you really are deep inside. Each missionary is unique. Each companion you had possessed different strengths and weaknesses though every companion had the role of missionary. You are no longer a full-time missionary. You will now take different roles as you return from your mission. People will ask you questions like, "What is your major?" or "What do you want to do with that?" or "What do you do for work?" You will naturally respond with "I'm a . . . fill in the blank with your current *role*." Never let your current *role* be confused with your *identity*.

Examples of core identity characteristics:
- Peacemaker
- Student
- Speaker
- Scientist
- Artist
- Influencer
- Leader
- Starter
- A people person
- Innovator
- An educated person
- Potentialist
- Mover and shaker
- Romantic
- Multipotentialite
- Believer
- Spiritual person
- Regulator
- Organizer
- Adventurer
- Discoverer

You could add the words "at heart" after any identity characteristic. You will rarely, if ever, mention your identity characteristics in a job interview or an introduction. Our society revolves around roles. Unless you are having a heart-to-heart conversation with someone, you will rarely talk about who you really are at heart. The important thing to remember is that you will need to become really clear about the characteristics of your core identity to discover and live your unique life mission.

Once you clarify your core identity characteristics, you will be more capable of looking at your life and figuring out a role that might complement your core identity. Some people use personality tests to figure these out. I think this can be helpful. A few that have helped me are the Myers-Briggs Test and the Color Code Personality Test. There are free versions of both of these online. In addition to these, I have a method that helps me to trust my gut and get clear about who I am. Here it is:

> **Step 1**. Find a comfortable place that will allow you to be undisturbed for at least an hour. Bring a snack if you have to. You may need to plan ahead so that you don't have anything pop up. Turn off all devices and bring your journal or whatever feels most comfortable for writing or typing your thoughts.

> **Step 2**. Draw a line down the middle of your paper if you are using a journal or create a table if you are using an electronic document. Write down what you believe the top ten personal achievements or accomplishments in your life. These are things you have done that *you personally* feel very proud of having accomplished. Make sure you number each one. Examples: Learned to play clarinet in sixth grade, kept a steady journal since I was ten years old, learned how to build a website, went on a mission, learned a foreign

language, graduated from high school, stayed out of debt, got accepted to my program, etc.

Step 3. Look at each one and ask yourself the question, "What does this say about the type of person I am?" or "Why did I do this?" or "Why was this a meaningful accomplishment for me?" Write the corresponding number and your response to these questions. Think about it and be true to your heart as you write. Why was it important for you to accomplish these things?

Step 4. Repeat step two, but instead of writing things you have accomplished, write down ten things that you want to accomplish in the next ten years. Make sure the things you write down are things that are personally meaningful to you.

Step 5. Look at each of these ten future accomplishments and answer the question, "What does this say about the type of person I want to become?" and "Why do I want to do this?" and "Why is this a meaningful accomplishment for me?"

After you have completed this exercise, you should be able to pick out some core identity characteristics.

Here is an example with just one from my life:

I graduated from university	I am a dedicated student. I love learning. I am a hard worker. This was meaningful to me because my mom and many of my siblings didn't graduate from university, and it feels good.
I want to travel the world with my camera	I want to be independent and financially stable enough to travel. I love to discover new cultures, religions, art and meet new people. I love adventure. This would be meaningful because I am an artist at heart.

You will be much happier and fulfilled in life if you align your academic study, jobs, careers—and as many roles you take on within those—with your core identity characteristics. The personality tests can help you see some of them. The above exercise can help you find more. Pray about this as well, and God will help you to see yourself more clearly.

The more you separate your roles from your core identity characteristics, the easier it will be to clarify your mission in life because you know the person you are at heart. Regardless of the roles you take on throughout your life, you will always be clear on who you are and why you are doing what you are doing. It's not bad to want to be a missionary again. You should always try to be a member missionary. However, I believe the returned missionaries who flourish the most are the ones who separate their role as a missionary from the characteristics of their core identity. They flourish because they can take these core characteristics and strengths and move forward in life stepping out of the role of a missionary and stepping into new roles. They understand that being a missionary was truly important, but the reason they were so happy is because they were using their core characteristics to be an amazing missionary.

People will always ask you if you have adjusted to the world yet after your mission. This makes me feel uncomfortable because it sounds like the expectation is to step into worldliness. It's as if you can't be truly acceptable as a returned missionary until you have stepped into worldliness again. This should not be so. Adjusting from the mission should never break the standards of the Church, full-time missionary or not. My idea of adjusting is not stepping into any form of worldliness. Instead, it is solidifying your core identity characteristics and stepping out of the role of full-time missionary into new roles. If you have done this, you can answer with confidence that you have adjusted.

Did you watch all the movies you missed while on the mission? Have you had your first kiss after the mission? Do you feel comfortable going by your first name again? All of these questions are personal, and the only thing you should focus on is if you are clear on your identity. If you are, go forward with confidence into the next role you will take on and disregard what everyone else says about your adjustment. That is between you and God, period.

No matter what roles you take on, your core identity is what will stay with you forever. Never forget that as you come home and seek to discover and *live* your personal life mission.

Chapter 2
One Size Doesn't Fit All

"Everybody is a genius. But if you judge a fish by its ability to climb a tree, it will live its whole life believing that it is stupid."

- Matthew Kelly

A symphony is beautiful because there are so many different instruments working together at once. No one would buy a piano if all it played were middle C. What makes piano music beautiful is the fact that there are eighty-eight unique keys that have a unique role in the masterpiece of the musician.

This world is like the symphony. We all have something different to contribute, and just because lawyers and stockbrokers can make a lot of money doesn't mean you are here to become one. Even if your whole family is artistic, it's okay to become a tax accountant if that is what your mission is. And just because your father, grandfather, and great-grandfather were all car dealers, doesn't mean you have to keep the family business going if your calling in life is to become a professional photographer.

We all have something a little different to offer. The beauty is that there are people for everything. Everyone fits perfectly somewhere. I have had critics (mostly the ones inside my head) that say "well, if everyone quits their desk job and starts a blog or travels the world to discover who they are, the economy will fail and the world will tumble into chaos." I agree with this. But I also don't think it would ever happen. I believe that not everyone will. I actually believe that some people feel called to office jobs. Some people actually find flow (see the chapter called "Find Your Flow") as a deli meat grinder, carpenter, or defense attorney. That is the beauty of it!

One size doesn't fit all, but everyone fits somewhere.

One of the most popular TED talks on the internet shows this very well. Sir Ken Robinson's speech (with over 29 million views when I wrote this) called "How School Kills Creativity" shows that one size most definitely does not fit all. But the "one size" that we are all supposed to fit into is that of university. The problem with that is that most university education programs are created to push the students out to get a job. Ken tells a story of Gillian Lynne. When she was a girl, she didn't fit the public education mold. She couldn't hold still in class as a child and just wasn't able to keep her attention on what the students were supposed to be learning. Her mother struggled to know what to do because the school administrators told her that she must have a learning disorder. Finally, Gillian's mother took her to a specialist and told him everything about how she struggled in school and was not focusing like all the other kids. After twenty minutes of explaining to the doctor all the things that were probably wrong with her, he went into the other room and turned on his radio. Upon hearing the music, Gillian immediately started to dance. The doctor looked over at Gillian's mother and said, "Mrs. Lynne Gillian isn't sick . . . she's a dancer. Take her to a dance school." Gillian was taken to a dance school and went on to be a brilliant dancer and the choreographer for *Cats* and *Phantom of the Opera*. Her brilliance has inspired millions, and she is a multi-millionaire.

> ". . . the whole system of public education around the world is a protracted process of university entrance. And the consequence is that many highly talented, brilliant, creative people think they're not because the thing they were good at at school wasn't valued, or was actually stigmatized." (Ken Robinson, "Do Schools Kill Creativity?" June 2006, TED.com)

You are a brilliant person, but it may not be in the way that the rest of the world (or even your mom) thinks. You may be one of those people who need to move and wiggle to learn. If that is the case, it is okay. One size does not fit all. You don't have to graduate from university to be successful or make money.

Don't grind off the beautiful edges of your square peg-ness to fit into someone else's round hole. Be yourself and be it well. One size does not fit all. Remember this as you seek to discover your life mission.

Chapter 3
Try on a Lot of Hats

"Don't be too timid and squeamish about your actions. All life is an experiment. The more experiments you make the better."

- Ralph Waldo Emerson

Amerca has evolved. There used to be one store in town. Now there are many, and within the many stores there are multiple brands, prices, and styles. We have a multitude of options to choose from. What a blessing to have so much to choose from! However, all these choices create anxiety. What kind of eggs to choose? White eggs? Cage free? Organic with no hormones? Omega 3 added? Once you choose the type, then you get to choose the brand. Which one is more environmentally friendly? Which one has more likes on their Facebook page? Boom decision made. Right? It is stressful to make decisions— not because having more options is bad—but because of the way our brain works. Our brain is programmed to be averse to a missed opportunity. I will talk more about this in the chapter called "Think Nike." For now, I will just tell you that having more choices, according to Dr. Barry Schwartz, makes us more stressed and therefore not as good at making decisions.

According to Barry Schwartz's theory about the paradox of choice, the regret of not having chosen all the options that were available to us will be greater than the excitement of the option we finally choose. The stress of potential regret will likely be greater than the joy of decision. And until you find your passion (what Ken Robinson calls your "element,") you will most likely be unsatisfied with your first (or even second) choice. So how do you avoid this when figuring out your calling in life?

Try on a lot of hats.

You may disagree with me and say that committing to one career and sticking to it is more virtuous. You may be right, but I would say (and so would research) that you will be significantly more satisfied with your chosen path *after* you have tried on lots of hats.

Do at least a handful of activities that you might not find yourself doing naturally. Volunteer a lot. Take an odd job. Get an internship in an unrelated field. Step down the corporate ladder a little so that you can step sideways. Apply for an interesting job in a field that is completely unrelated to your educational degree. You may not get the job, but you will have some really interesting interviews.

You may just find at the end of your seemingly pointless journey that you are much more satisfied with the choice you would have made at first. In fact, research shows that after you have tried on a lot of hats and then come back to the original hat, you will be much more satisfied with the original hat than if you would have just kept that hat on with the possibility of all the other hats.

Some might say that is stupid. Maybe so, but you will be happier, and happier people are more productive and successful. Harvard professor and famed happiness lecturer Shawn Achor shows this in his book called *The Happiness Advantage*. He said, "positive brains have a biological advantage over brains that are neutral or negative," and the people who are more positive will be more successful and will perform significantly higher than those who are negative. So when we are in our "hat one" job and we are constantly ruminating over the fact that we never tried our hand as a NASA intern to become an astronaut, we will be much less successful and productive in that job than if we had given a few of the options a try. It may take longer, but I guarantee you will be happier and more productive when you settle with hat five or hat six.

If you are still critical of the research above, you can do your own little research project. Interview five to ten people who are fixed in their chosen profession. Ask them these questions:

1. How long have you worked at your current job?
2. What do you love about your job?
3. What do you not love about your job?
4. Is the job you have now your idea of the ideal job?
5. (If appropriate) what would the perfect job look like to you?
6. (If appropriate) What keeps you from moving over to doing that?
7. How many jobs did you have before you landed this one?
8. Where do you see yourself in five years? Ten years?
9. What advice can you give me?

The best thing that ever happened to me was getting fired from a "solid job" that I was not passionate about so that I could make an iPhone app and start an SEO business. Now I love internet entrepreneurship, and I am going to get my masters in positive psychology to strengthen and amplify my voice and keep sharing principles of the science of happiness. These are my passions. If I were still at that solid job I got fired from three years ago, I would be getting a great paycheck and stock options in a company that was offered 500 million to sell. It would be really cool to talk about, and I would be totally miserable.

Don't be miserable. Try on more hats.

Chapter 4
Get Outside Your Comfort Zone

"Do not go where the path may lead, go instead where there is no path, and leave a trail."- Ralph Waldo Emerson

If you do things the way you have always done them, you will get what you have always gotten. If you want to accomplish something you have never accomplished, you need to do things that you have never done, in ways you have never done them.

You will have to get outside of your comfort zone.

Too many dreams are aborted by fear before they are even born.

The main character from *Strictly Ballroom,* Fran, was right when she said:

"A life lived in fear is a life half lived."

The fastest way to dry up the roots of your potential is to allow fear to dominate your thinking and never to get outside your comfort zone. What you must remember is that fear comes from believing something that is not true. Anytime you have a fear, you must increase your knowledge of truth and determine what you are allowing yourself to believe that is *not* true. Every major success, every major hero has had to overcome fear. And *anyone* can overcome fear with *truth*.

So take a big dose of truth, put on your Spanish red dress or your sparkly man-vest and get out on the dance floor and do the Paso Doble!

Overcome your fears. Get outside your comfort zone. You will learn a lot as you do this.

In a moving speech, Gordon B. Hinckley states: "One of the great tragedies we witness almost daily is the tragedy of men of high aim and low achievement. Their motives are noble. Their proclaimed ambition is praiseworthy. Their capacity is great. But their discipline is weak. They succumb to indolence. Appetite robs them of will." (*And Peter Went Out and Wept Bitterly,* Gordon B. Hinckley, April 1979.)

Indolence is the epitome of staying in your comfort zone. You have an amazing potential. You have a high aim. Don't let your appetite or apathy rob you of the greatest life you could live. Get outside your comfort zone and step into the zone of greatness. Commit to something. Grab the bull by the horns. When you do, you'll find a new tribe there to support you. A tribe full of other people who have stepped out of their comfort zones and become something great.

Research shows that regret of things that *you actually did* is much easier to overcome than regret of things you *never* did. See more about this in the chapter called "Think Nike."

Step out of the comfort. Step into your best self. You'll be glad you did.

Chapter 5
Seek a Problem to Solve
and a Question to Answer

"And take upon us the mystery of things,
As if we were God's spies." - William Shakespeare

Maybe you watched the scene in *The Truman Show* where Truman Burbank is in his elementary school class and states that he wants to be a discoverer. His teacher then looks at him and says, "Why? Everything has already been discovered."

Sometimes we might feel this way as we seek to find our mission. We think we want to be something great, but to us it seems like everything worth inventing has already been invented and everything significant has already been discovered. There is nothing left to discover anymore. Why even try? Besides, even if there are problems to solve and questions to answer, there are probably ten other people who are smarter and who have more money that are way ahead of me.

Well, I'm here to tell you *that is wrong*. You are unique. You are the only one like you in the whole world, and you have something to contribute that no other person can. There are questions that *only you* can answer and problems that *only you* can solve. When Truman finally got the courage to explore his world, he found the truth, and you will find the truth as well.

By the year 1666, had anyone ever seen an apple fall from a tree? Obvious answer. Millions had seen this happen. Then why was the law of gravity not discovered until this time? What was so different about this 1666 apple? Nothing was different about the apple. The difference was Sir Isaac Newton. Newton wasn't the first person to get hit on the head by an apple, but he was the first one to put two and two together (more like putting *Opticks* and *Principia* together).

You are no different than Newton.

You can do something that no other person can. So look at the problems of the world around you and start looking for answers to the questions that your world needs answered. One man who changed the world forever, Steve Jobs, said this:

> "Life can be much broader once you discover one simple fact - and that is - everything around you that you call life was made up by people that were no smarter than you. And you can change it, you can influence it, you can build your own things that other people can use. Once you learn that, you'll never be the same again." (From PBS' *One Last Thing* documentary, which aired on TV in 2011)

There are problems in your community, in the nation and around the world that require people to stand up and solve. Here are a few more from around the world:

- Human trafficking and slavery (yep, they still exist)
- Easy access to pornography
- New laws and regulations that affect religious liberty and marriage
- Multiple natural disasters that happen around the world every year
- The decline and attack of traditional marriage and family
- Lack of good education
- The marriage of technology and education
- Bullying and violence in schools

- Cyberbullying
- Reintegration of prisoners back into society
- The increase of mental illness and suicide rates
- The leading causes of death: CHD and cancer always top the list
- Medical malpractice
- Alcoholism and drug abuse
- Orphans
- Hunger
- Genetically modified foods
- Pesticides killing bees
- Internet trolls / digital aggression
- Hygiene
- Sustainable energy
- Droughts or the lack of clean water
- Lack of good leadership in communities, states and nations

If you want to know about more problems, watch the news. If you want to learn more about problems *and* possible solutions to those problems, watch some TED talks. In addition to problems to solve, there are also a myriad of questions to answer. Some might argue against this pursuit, but many problems are solved by answering questions.

Come up with some questions. What questions fascinated you as a child? What fascinates you now? Basic questions like "why is the sky blue?" have motivated discoveries that have changed the world.

Everyone has questions. Google has become one of the most successful companies in the world because people ask questions. Some months they have received 4.7 billion searches in one day. But remember that Google isn't the source. *We are the source* that Google indexes and points to. The millions upon millions of websites that people like you and me have built and published are the source of the information, not Google. Google wouldn't have a viable business without everyone else's knowledge and information.

You are a unique person who has been placed in a unique position in this world. You can answer questions that may have been asked in a way that no other person on earth can. So start answering questions and make the answers known to the world. Millions of people can benefit from your unique answer to a question. Don't underestimate your unique perspective.

Maybe every inch of the earth has been discovered, but there are millions of questions to answer and millions of problems to solve.

Go be the answer.

Chapter 6
Don't Live Someone Else's Dream

"To thine own self be true and it must follow as the night the day thou canst not be false to any man." - William Shakespeare

If J.K. Rowling stopped when her idea was turned down by multiple publishers, we might have never known Harry Potter. William Wilberforce never would have taken down the slave trade in Great Britain seeking the approval of others. Instead of becoming an artist, Michelangelo would have become a businessman on the advice of his father, and we would never have seen the matchless Pieta or the incredible paintings in the Sistine Chapel. King Agrippa may have actually become a Christian. Walt Disney may have just given up after being turned down by 300 investors, and Disney World may have drifted into the void of ideas that never happen.

Don't seek approval of others. Don't live someone else's dream. Stay true to the vision within you.

Steve Jobs said at one of his most popular speeches:

> Your time is limited, *so don't waste it living someone else's life. Don't be trapped by dogma - which is living with the results of other people's thinking. Don't let the noise of other's opinions drown out your own inner voice.* And most important, have the courage to follow your heart and intuition. They somehow already know what you truly want to become. Everything else is secondary. (Stanford Report, June 14, 2005, emphasis added.)

Jobs' advice is crucial to remember when seeking to find your mission in life. *Don't live someone else's dream.* Don't get trapped.

Live your own life. Make your own goals. If your dad is a doctor and wants you to be a doctor, but you want to be a photographer, be a photographer! Don't live your dad's vision of success. You don't need their approval to be happy.

Consider Patricia Holland's counsel:

> "We are becoming so concerned about having perfect figures, or straight A's, or professional status . . . that we are being torn from our true selves. We often worry so much about pleasing and performing for others that we lose our own uniqueness, that full and relaxed acceptance of ourselves as a person of worth and individuality." (Patricia T. Holland, "The Soul's Center" [13 January 1987], *BYU 1986–87 Devotional and Fireside Speeches*, 84.)

And the counsel of Sharon Samuelson:

> "The world in which we live today tells us that our sense of worth is based upon what is seen or accomplished. We are measured by possessions and wealth, physical appearance and dress styles, social status and achievements. Too many of us strive to gain acceptance using these standards, trying to enhance the perception of our worth by those who are part of our lives as well as those who view us from afar. *If we are not careful, we can let others determine and establish our standards and feelings of self-worth. We can become someone else's image of success rather than our own.*" (Sharon Samuelson, "A Place Within His Heart", BYU Devotional given January 10, 2006.)

Don't become someone else's vision of success. Live your own life. Be your own master. To thine own self be true.

Chapter 7
Hop a Plane and Get out of Dodge.

"Sometimes you find yourself in the middle of nowhere, and sometimes in the middle of nowhere, you find yourself."- Anonymous

Inside of us, we have a desire to overcome injustice, to fight against ignorance and to eliminate prejudice around us. It is a part of our soul. We are all born with the desire for freedom. Look at history. Whenever people are in bondage, they either fight for their freedom, or they escape to become free. Freedom is a critical part of our spiritual DNA.

When we travel, we feel free. Not only are we physically moving away from the things that seem to cause us to feel in any way bound, but we experience other people, cultures, religions, and perspectives. We are endowed with a new set of lenses through which we see our own world.

Most importantly, we can see ourselves more clearly than we ever have before.

If you are from Idaho and have never left Idaho your whole life, it will amaze you the first time you go to Amman, Jordan and see a man praying on a rug next to a car stopped on the side of the interstate highway. If you grew up in a small Kenyan town where you have to walk two miles to get clean water, the first time you witness an American water balloon fight in the summer will shock you.

I will tell you of an experience I had when traveling the world with my wife. We spent a night in Wadi Musa, Jordan (the home of the famous ancient Petra ruins seen in Indiana Jones) during Ramadan. The taxi driver who drove us from the border told us he would pick us up the next day to take us back to the border for the same price. We told him we needed to go earlier and that we would find a different ride. He said to come with him anyway. A little bit annoyed, I just said okay so that he would leave us alone and we could get going. As an American, I just assumed that this was no big deal and that I would carry on and find a better deal and an earlier ride after we hiked the Siq slot canyon. So we did (we even left him a tip and a thank you note).

Well, about halfway back to the border the next day, our *new* taxi driver gets a call on his phone from our *former* angry taxi driver asking for Andy. On the phone, he threatened me and told me that I didn't keep my word. I told him that I had never signed anything and that we needed to leave earlier to make our bus from Eilat to

Jerusalem. This just enraged him even more, and he said he would meet us at the border with the Jordanian police. *What?!* Long story short, we barely made it past the money-bribed border patrolmen carrying machine guns with no money, no phone, and no way to get to the bus stop or even to an ATM. We were stuck in no man's land between two countries who hate each other.

At the border in line with us, we also met the most friendly people who also just happened to be traveling the world. They noticed that we spoke English and that we were in trouble. After we had gotten our passports stamped, they offered to let us ride in their tiny little rental car until Jerusalem. What a miracle! And this car ride produced the most interesting four-hour conversation we have ever had in our lives.

One nineteen-year-old girl from England, who was Jewish.

One twenty-year-old boy from England, who was Anglican.

One twenty-one-year-old girl from Canada, who was Eastern Orthodox.

And Stacie and me - two Mormons.

We all found ourselves lost by the Dead Sea trying to make it to Jerusalem together after being given a dose of injustice and corruption at the border. I don't think anyone could ever replicate this experience. It was so unique. We were all there for different reasons, but we all had one thing in common: humanity. We all ate food, needed to go to the bathroom, and appreciated a good laugh.

That travel experience taught me truckloads about myself that I never could get by just reading a book like this. It helped me to solidify for myself who I am and *why* I am. It gave me multiple differing perspectives from other people who were also solidifying their idea of themselves. It also showed me what I *didn't* want to become (a desperate man corrupted by money) as well as what I *did* want to become (a kind human being showing compassion to others in need).

It stirred in me so many questions to answer. It made me appreciate my fellow English-speakers, but it made me feel compassion for the man at the border who was so desperate for money that he would sacrifice his integrity for it. It made me appreciate true kindness. It showed me that honesty may actually be a cultural thing but solidified the desire inside of me to hold strong to the morals I know to be right, even if they aren't supported by my own culture.

I saw who I was, and who I wasn't. I was given an inoculation for what I never wanted to see in myself, and I saw a glimpse of what I wanted to become.

As you seek to discover your mission in life, you will need a fresh view of you. A new perspective. A view of yourself that you can only get by getting out of Dodge.

Traveling the world will give that to you.

So travel the world. It will open your eyes. You will see things you never had supposed. And this new perspective may just be the very ingredient you need to discover your calling in life. Not only to see the world more clearly *but to see yourself more clearly.*

As you see yourself more clearly, your mission will emerge.

Now go start planning your trip!

Author's Note: Now go search "Move, Travel Video" on YouTube to inspire you as you pack!

Chapter 8
Find Some Grandparents

"What is it about grandparents that is so lovely?
I'd like to say that grandparents are God's gifts to children.
And if they can but see, hear and feel what these people have to give,
they can mature at a fast rate." - Bill Cosby

On your quest to know your mission in life, look to your grandparents. If yours have passed on, look around and adopt some. You'll be glad you did. They will inject you with perspective you can find nowhere else. Just take my grandma for example. She is 96 (May 2015), and she still gets on Facebook and likes my posts. But she also was around when Mark Zuckerberg's mom was in diapers. She has lived through the effects of two world wars, the Great Depression, Vietnam, the Cold War, the Cuban Missile Crisis, the MLK and JFK assassinations, the race to the moon and the Apollo 13 mission, the Challenger Disaster, the Berlin Wall coming down, September 11, seventeen presidents of the United States with all their ups and downs, ten Mormon prophets have stood as she listened to General Conference and over a million full-time LDS missionaries have served and come home during her lifetime. She has seen a lot. She has been there and back again. And she is still going strong. Just last year she traveled to Jerusalem and rode a camel as you can see in the picture below. She is an inspiration to me and there is much to learn about our calling from our elders.

There are plenty of grandparents who would welcome you asking their advice and probably give you a plate of cookies and some fresh homemade jam to take home.

Statistically, older people are happier. The data shows it. Laura Carstensen, the director of the Stanford Center for Longevity, who is well known for her life-span theory of motivation (the socioemotional selectivity theory) gave a fascinating TED talk about getting old. You could just Google it and watch the video, or just read the highlights here:

> "Aging brings some rather remarkable improvements -- increased knowledge, expertise -- and emotional aspects of life improve. That's right, older people are happy. They're happier than middle-aged people, and younger people certainly. Study after study is coming to the same conclusion . . . stress, worry, anger all decrease with age.

> "In our study, they are more positive, but they're also more likely than younger people to experience mixed emotions -- sadness at the same time you experience happiness; you know, that tear in the eye when you're smiling at a friend. And other research has shown that older people seem to engage with sadness more comfortably.

They're more accepting of sadness than younger people are. And we suspect that this may help to explain why older people are better than younger people at solving hotly-charged emotional conflicts and debates. Older people can view injustice with compassion, but not despair . . .

"As we age, our time horizons grow shorter and our goals change. When we recognize that we don't have all the time in the world, we see our priorities most clearly. We take less notice of trivial matters. We savor life. We're more appreciative, more open to reconciliation. We invest in more emotionally important parts of life, and life gets better, so we're happier day-to-day." (Laura Carstensen, "Older People Are Happier", TED.com)

Carstensen's data makes me want to hang out more with the elderly. They have seen it all and are more adept to the challenges of life. They have wisdom you need, not only because they have more experience, but because they are more capable of looking past the fleeting emotional issues of a situation that to us might seem extremely important but to them is something that they have seen come and go a hundred times.

Sink your teeth into the wisdom of the aged. They will help you see yourself more clearly, show you things that you never thought of, and upgrade your personal experience with the breadth of their perspective.

Look to some grandparents in your quest for your personal mission in life.

Chapter 9
Seek for Flow

"What man actually needs is not a tensionless state but rather the striving and struggling for some goal worthy of him."

- Victor Frankl

D o you ever find yourself so totally immersed in what you are doing that you lose track of time? You look down at your phone and realize that hours have passed, and you missed dinner? When does this loss of time and complete engagement typically happen for you? This could apply to a water skier who can't stop gliding across perfectly glassy water or a cellist immersed in the complexity of a symphony.

Flow, or complete engagement, is the precise balance between anxiety and boredom. It's where you are using a natural skill that you possess while at the same time being challenged in this skill. When this happens, we lose track of time, feel less physical pain, perceive the world differently, don't care what others think about us, and feel like we are in control. When we experience flow, we are happier (*Flow*, Mihaly Csikszentmihalyi).

So, when you sit and brainlessly watch Netflix have a YouTube binge session, you may find some satisfaction in what you are watching, but you are not in a flow state because to find flow, you must be challenged with some skill that you have. On the other hand, driving a car with a manual transmission for the first time in your life in front of a $75,000 sports car going up Lombard Street in San Francisco is too challenging to enjoy. Instead of enjoyment, you feel anxiety. Flow is the perfect balance between these two opposites. When we find this balance, we experience flow.

Why would finding flow be important as we seek to find our unique life mission? I think that those who don't make enough effort really to find flow in what they do with their life will eventually burn out. Whether that burnout comes from stress and anxiety or boredom, they will eventually quit. This is evident in many businesses.

Some businesses focus on strengths in their approach and have found that this increases productivity and creativity. Businesses that don't lose money. When employees find more flow by engaging in their work based on their strengths, not only do the individuals flourish but the businesses do as well.

> Less than 30% of employees are engaged at work, costing $300 billion each year. The likelihood of an employee being engaged is 9% in organizations that don't focus on strengths, and is 73% in organizations that do. (State of Global Workplace, Gallup '10).

How does that apply to you? Well, the majority of you will be busy at work for a good portion of every week, a good portion of your entire life. If you find flow while at work, your entire life will be filled with so much more happiness and wellbeing. If you just go to work to make money and you have no satisfaction in what you do every single day, it will be really difficult for you to want to move forward for too long. You may stick it out for a few years, but in the end you will burn out.

The great thing is that you get to choose what you do!

So as you seek to find your life mission (and hopefully your work can go hand in hand with what your mission is), seek for that flow experience. The activity that challenges your natural skill to the point where you enjoy it and get lost doing it. Where you lose track of time and you don't want to go home from work.

Though it may take longer for you to find flow in your work, I believe it is worth it. Your job doesn't have to be pure flow, but why not get paid to do something that causes you to lose track of time?

And not all people will find flow in their line of work. No matter what your circumstance, you can still explore different activities to find where you experience flow.

The more often you experience flow, the closer you might be to your unique life mission. Remember that your life mission is not going to be something without challenges. In fact, if you believe you have found your mission in some activity or line of work that doesn't challenge your natural gifts and talents at all, I would double check yourself. Your mission will challenge you to become something greater than you are. And you will enjoy the challenge.

Find your flow. Find that enjoyable challenge. You are worth it.

Chapter 10

Think Less about Pie
and More about Loaves and Fishes

"I am come that they might have life, and that they might have it more abundantly." - Jesus Christ (John 10:10)

On our honeymoon, Stacie and I found ourselves in the city of Tiberias on the northwest shore of the Sea of Galilee. Our local friend Eddie invited us to have dinner with him at one of his favorite restaurants in Galilee. Eddie is one of the most interesting people I have ever met in my life. He is a multilingual fifty-something-year-old man who wears glasses and only has the use of one arm. As we sat down to eat with Eddie, he offered to buy our meal. This was a blessing because we were on a tight budget while traveling the world. What we didn't realize was that he not only offered to buy our dinner, but he paid for us to try one of everything in the entire restaurant! Plate by plate, the entire menu piled up on our table and Eddie said with a chuckle in his voice, "The best way to find out what you like is to buy the whole restaurant!" This experience changed the way I see the world around me. Some might say that this was wasteful and that there are starving children in Africa; indeed, we could not even make a dent on all the food that was on our table, but I have thought about this dinner over and over because it painted a real-life picture for me of the principle of abundance.

Too many of us think in terms of pieces of the pie. If *you* get a piece, then *I don't* get a piece, and there are only so many pieces to go around before it all runs out. I believe this paradigm limits the potential inside of us because it makes the world seem cold and bitter.

I like to think of things in terms of loaves and fishes than in terms of pieces of the pie. When Jesus performed the miracle of the loaves and fishes, He was teaching us something very important. Surely this miracle taught us about God's love and compassion for a hungering crowd of five-thousand. More importantly though, it also taught us that He is a God who wants us to understand the *abundance mentality.*

It wasn't a coincidence to me that this dinner experience happened just minutes away from where the loaves and fishes were multiplied to feed five-thousand. And I believe God wanted me to have a taste (no pun intended) of the abundance mentality that He has.

As we seek to discover our unique life mission, we need to develop an abundance mentality.

When we try to discover our life mission with a scarcity paradigm, we will never find it. If you look around you with scarcity lenses over your eyes, it would look as if the world is against you and that all opportunities have already been snatched up before you could ever get to them. With a scarcity mentality, you will see others as competition who you must conquer. Seeing the world this way will plant bitterness in your heart every time anyone else has a success in life. When someone else celebrates because they have discovered their life mission, you will feel jealousy instead of joy. Instead of shouting out in celebration, you will silently despise them for taking what could have been yours.

I have been guilty of this in my life. I came home from my mission and for years I felt bitterness when my mission friends got married before I did or when my classmates landed a great job or got into a great graduate program or made it big in business before me. I was looking through the lens of scarcity. I believed that because there were only so many great jobs, or amazing young women or unique opportunities, that they had all been snatched up, and God had moved on without me because I wasn't fast enough or smart enough to get one of the pieces of the pie. I literally believed that God basically forgot about those who weren't the best, brightest, and most attractive. And I wasn't one of them.

This simply is not the case.

God has not forgotten you. You may feel like you are less important than the other ten-thousand returned missionaries who just got home from their missions, but you aren't. God has enough time and attention for you and enough power to help you and enough wisdom to guide you. If you believe in the miracle of the loaves and fishes, then you believe in a God who has the mental bandwidth to help you discover your unique life mission and the power to help you carry it out. That is the God I believe in. The type of Father who orders the whole restaurant just so that I know what it feels like to experience abundance.

As I mentioned earlier in the book, one size does not fit all and there are opportunities galore for every single person in the world.

In the last chapter of the gospel of John, this principle is confirmed for me. Jesus is gone and His apostles have gone back to their homes in Galilee. Peter goes fishing out on the Sea of Galilee with the disciples, and while fishing he heard a voice coming from shore. It was the Savior. He said to them, "Children, have ye any meat?" They hadn't caught anything at all. And then He said, "Cast the net on the right side of the ship and ye shall find." When they did, they were not able to pull the net in because there were so many fishes.

This was not the first time this had happened and it isn't the last. We are all like Peter. We come home from our missions and start doing the things we know how to do. But too often it feels like we fish all night and don't catch a thing. Maybe we look around at other fishermen around us and think, "Oh man, I should have gotten up earlier," or "I should have gone to the other side of the lake. It looks like those fishermen are raking in the fish," or "Why do all the other boats look nicer than mine?" or "I'm not even fit to catch fish in this life. There just isn't any room for me here to have success." The equivalent of these thoughts have all crossed through my head as I have "gone fishing" in my quest to find my mission in life. Despite all of these defeating thoughts, I believe in the God of the loaves and fishes. And if Jesus can tell Peter where to cast his net to find fish, He can tell *you* where to cast *your* net to find success and happiness in your life now.

Never forget that if you listen for His voice, He will tell you where to cast your net so that you can find anything you seek including a spouse, a career, or your unique life mission. When we have the abundance mentality, we are happy at the success of others and we are more able to find our unique life mission. Remember that God can make miracles of abundance happen in your life as you seek to discover your unique life mission. Listen for His call after you come home and He will tell you where to cast your nets.

Chapter 11

Wipe off Your Yester-self
and Stay Out of Hell

"Today I begin a new life. Today I shed my old skin which hath, too long, suffered the bruises of failure and the wounds of mediocrity."

- The Scroll Marked I (Og Mandino)

Qualtrics is still one of the most successful startup companies in Utah's "Silicon Slopes." In just a few years, it went from the basement of a BYU professor to being offered a half-billion to sell. I was employee number thirteen. I loved being a part of something that was growing like crazy. The culture was fun and fresh, the management was good. We had food to eat at the office and free clothes and swag at least once a quarter. I'm a people person, and I really enjoyed working with amazing people who were using technology to accelerate their research. When I started to believe that I might work with Qualtrics for the rest of my life, everything changed.

I can still remember when my manager walked me to a soundproof room where he sat me down and said, "Andy, this meeting is to tell you that today was your last day at Qualtrics. We can gather your things, or we can escort you to your desk, and you can pick them up. Your accounts have been deactivated already. Do you have any questions?" I was so shocked by what was happening that I didn't really know what to say or what questions to ask. Just days before, this same manager had assigned me to work on a huge overhaul project that would benefit thousands of academics and Qualtrics users. I helped launch some of the biggest surveys for some of the biggest corporate and academic clients and developed a research tool that has been requested by many academics all over the world. I was confused because I was under the impression that I was an asset to the company, and yet I wasn't enough of an asset to keep me on or even give me fair warning before letting me go. Despite all of the shock, humiliation, and disappointment, this was one of the best things that ever happened to me.

My manager, who used to work for Google, also told me something that I will never forget. He said, "Andy, it hurts, but it's okay, and it happened to me before. You'll be fine, and it will be even better." Looking back on this event years later, I realize how right my manager was. Even though Qualtrics was a great experience, I really didn't want to be there. Whether I was consciously putting off those vibes or not, the message that I didn't want to be there was clear enough to these managers that they let me go. And I am so glad because I was forced to decide what I really wanted. And because I was humbled, I was able to take a good look at myself and decide what I wanted to keep and what I wanted to wipe off as I went into the next chapter of life.

You may not get let go from an amazing job like me, but you will have many opportunities to create a new idea of who you are. One of those times is right after your mission. You get to recreate the self that you want to become. You are no longer a full-time missionary, so what are you now? Who are you now? As an undergraduate student at BYU, I jumped from one ward to the next year after year. I loved this feeling because I got to recreate myself each time. I could keep what I loved and wipe off what I didn't love about myself. One year I even went by a different name and instead of telling people that my name was Andy I introduced myself as Drew (my full name is Andrew). It was really interesting as I paired my new chosen name with the new self I was taking on. Though it got a little confusing for my old friends, it felt good.

Like I mention in the first chapter of this book, it is important at crucial crossroads in your life to take a step back and take a look at the self you are becoming. Don't be afraid to wipe off pieces of yourself from yesterday and replace them with the better self you want to be today. It helps to surround yourself with greatness as you do this (see chapter 14). In fact it is necessary to surround yourself with people who will *let you be new*. Otherwise it will probably be really easy to get sucked back into the self you have established with people who don't let you become something better or something new.

My wife and I had made an agreement before we were married. We promised each other to let each other be new as often as we desired to be new. This has been one of the most important agreements of our marriage. You will rise or fall over time as you become a better and better person across the decades of decisions that you will make. And whether you realize it or not, you are becoming something. Each choice you make is like a brick, and the city of the self is being built whether you are aware of it or not. I believe it is critical to take a step back and see if you like the city you are building. If not, you may have to demolish a few brick walls before they become more solid buildings. It is good to do this often over the years until you get it the way you want it. Add bricks to buildings you want to build. Take bricks down where you don't want them. Those who do not deliberately build will at some point look at their city and find that there are lofty, solidified buildings they really don't want there. It is much easier to take those buildings down when they are merely a few stacks of bricks or even when the scaffolding is still up. It becomes much harder after they are fully constructed and even have residents living in them, metaphorically speaking. C.S. Lewis taught this principle masterfully:

> Now there are a good many things which would not be worth bothering about if I were going to live only seventy years, but which I had better bother about very seriously if I am going to live for ever. Perhaps my bad temper or my jealousy are gradually getting worse--so gradually that the increase in seventy years will not be very noticeable. But it might be absolute hell in a million years: in fact, if

42

Christianity is true, Hell is the precisely correct technical term for what it would be." (Mere Christianity, p. 74).

If you aren't deliberately building heaven within you, you are allowing hell to be built. And the best way to build your heaven is to take a step back to wipe off your yester-self and add bricks to your heavenly city.

Please don't go to hell (or become a living hell). Wipe off your yesterdays. Be okay with a new you. The best you.

Chapter 12
Look to Your Roots

"Some time in the spring of 1856, President Young put his hands on my head and set me apart to make my calling the growing of trees, shrubs and etc." - Charles Henry Oliphant (first official Utah horticulturist)

C harles Henry Oliphant has an interesting story. He grew up in New York, was abandoned by his father before he was born, and he lost his mother at a young age. He didn't even know his real last name until later in life. He trekked across the undeveloped trails from the East to Utah with the early settlers. He eventually became the first horticulturist in Utah, being assigned by the founder of Utah, Brigham Young. 159 years later, Lucas Henry Proctor, my brother (named after Charles Henry Oliphant) has become a horticulturist and arborist and loves every minute of it. You can't be around Lucas without hearing something about plants. Lucas has always just felt drawn to horticulture, and he is even prouder of the story of Charles Henry Oliphant because they share this heritage.

Even though your purpose will probably be different from your mom or dad, you may find that deep within your blood there was an ancestor (like Charles Henry Oliphant) that gravitated toward something that you also gravitate toward now. Do some family history research and figure out what made your ancestors tick. What was their motivation? Where were they at your age? What were they doing? They may just pay you a visit to help you out in your journey.

Not only will looking to your roots help you with figuring out your life mission, but it will also help you to overcome opposition when you step forward into that mission. A *New York Times* article highlighted research showing that the more children know about their family's history the stronger their sense of control over their lives and the higher their self-esteem. This knowledge of their family turned out to be the best single predictor of a child's emotional health and happiness. Another study in the article showed that those who have what they called a "strong intergenerational self" who were familiar with their family narrative of sticking together across the ups and downs had more self-confidence because they knew they were a part of something bigger than themselves. (*New York Times*, "The Family Stories that Bind Us", NYT, March 15, 2013). So even if you don't end up doing what your great great grandpa did, you will at least know that you come from a line of people who have overcome opposition, and you will be stronger as you move toward your goals and dreams in life.

If you don't know your family narrative, get to know it. Talk to your oldest living relatives and ask them to tell you stories about them and others in your family who went through really hard things, but who overcame those things. If you have no living relatives older than you, find the records that exist about them. If none of that exists, create your own family narrative starting now. The important thing is to associate yourself with something with noble beginnings. Remember where you came from.

No matter how few records exist of your family narrative, you have a noble narrative. Boyd K. Packer said this well:

"You are a child of God. He is the father of your spirit. Spiritually you are of noble birth, the offspring of the King of Heaven. Fix that truth in your mind and hold to it. However many generations in your mortal ancestry, no matter what race or people you represent, the pedigree of your spirit can be written on a single line. You are a child of God!" (Boyd K. Packer, "To Young Women and Men", CR, May 1989).

Spiritually you have the greatest narrative of all. You fought in the battle between good and evil. You were on the good side. You kept your first estate, and you chose to come to earth. You were on God's side then, and you are still on it now. This is a winning team that has a very strong narrative. This heritage is something that you can always hold on to.

As you look to your roots, you will be able to plug into the collective strength of the great men and women of the past who share your blood and your spiritual heritage. This strength will boost you forward not only with clarity into what your life mission is but with greater self-confidence as you implement that mission in your life.

Chapter 13
Trust Your Gut, Literally

"You can't connect the dots looking forward; you can only connect them looking backwards. So you have to trust that the dots will somehow connect in your future. You have to trust in something - your gut, destiny, life, karma, whatever. This approach has never let me down, and it has made all the difference in my life." - Steve Jobs

As a student in Jerusalem, I fell in love with a girl in my program. Our travel-study program took us from Jerusalem to the Pyramids of Egypt to the ruins of Petra to the Sea of Galilee. We got to watch the sunset over the Old City every evening from the BYU Jerusalem Center for almost four months. We had some very romantic opportunities to say the least. Our first kiss was on the shores of where Jesus walked on water. I thought that we were meant for each other. A few weeks after we had returned from Jerusalem, and we were back to the grind of everyday life, she said she wanted to talk to me. I didn't think as much about it, and I loved talking to her, so I grabbed us some Einstein's Bagels with the best cream cheese and picked her up. We went to the parking lot at the base of the trail that goes up to the big Y that is on the mountain overlooking Provo, UT. As we started to eat these scrumptious bagels, she turned to me and said: "Andy, I'm having a really hard time saying this, but I wrote you a note to explain how I feel." The air quickly changed from warm to stiff, and there was an invisible wall that went up between us without any words said. I read the note. It was obvious that she was breaking up with me. I started the car and drove her home. Both of us are very happily married to other people now, and the only reason I think about that experience these days is because of how quickly I lost my appetite. Einstein's Bagels are one of my favorite things to eat! Especially with their amazing whipped cream cheese. And no matter how good that was, my stomach said no and I didn't eat for a while after that experience. It was a hard breakup. And the bagels went bad before I could eat them.

The reason I bring this up isn't to show my gratitude for not having developed an aversion to Einstein's Bagels. It is to illustrate the connection between your gut and your brain. Your gastrointestinal tract is amazingly intertwined with your brain and in turn with your thoughts and emotions. It is amazing to think that the same types of cells that allow us to create a thought or feel an emotion in our brain are found in our gut. There are one hundred million nerve cells in the small intestine alone! In addition to the cells, there are chemicals called neurotransmitters that help make communication between these cells possible. One neurotransmitter that helps us to feel positive emotions like pleasure, joy, and relief is created almost primarily in our gut. That neurotransmitter is serotonin. Over 95% of the body's serotonin is produced in the bowel (*The Second Brain* by Dr. Michael Gershon, pp. xii, 15).

To me it would be a bit odd to think that in addition to all the muscular and structural cells of the small intestine, there are a hundred million nerve cells only to help us in the simple process of passing gas. I believe, and so do many current researchers, that the gut has more to offer than converting a bowl of cereal into a little brown pile each day. The gut is the only system that doesn't need direction from the central nervous system to do its job, but the brain takes into account quite a bit of information from the gut. Signals from the gut can reach the parts of the brain that are responsible for self-awareness, emotion, morality, fear, memory, and motivation (See *Gut* by Guilia Enders, MD, p. 126). For the purposes of this chapter, we won't start to get into the billions of gut flora (bacteria and fungi) that are also swimming around in our gut "talking" to each other and "talking" to us.

So when people say "trust your gut" or "I just have a gut feeling about this," that statement is much more profound than they might think. There may be more brain-gut interaction between your mind and your gut than you would have ever imagined. Time will tell as more data on this subject emerges, but for now we can be sure that processes similar to cognition are going on in our gut, every hour of every day. (*See LDS Footnote below)

When you get a gut feeling about something, trust it. Your gut literally knows more than you might think and because it is directly linked to areas of our subconscious mind. It may send you a message that you can't consciously make sense of but that just *feels* better to you. Trust that feeling as you are making decisions about your unique life mission. And if you have a bad gut feeling about something, you're not crazy. I believe it is because your conscious mind can't grasp what your subconscious mind is remembering, so you just get a bad gut feeling. Don't push that gut feeling aside (unless you just ate an entire order of deep fried chicken and a super-sized milkshake). If you get a tummy ache when you are about to take a huge financial risk, marry someone you don't feel right about, or take a higher paying job you aren't passionate about, know that you aren't crazy. You might just be getting a message communicated from your subconscious mind to your conscious mind, through your gut.

And above the vagus nerve connection between the gut and the brain, you also have a direct connection to a network that is much wiser than your gut, and that is the connection you get when you actively receive the Holy Ghost. As the Savior said, "The comforter . . . the Holy Ghost, whom the Father will send in my name, he shall teach you all things, and bring all things to your remembrance." (John 14:26). And Moroni says, "By the power of the Holy Ghost, ye may know the truth of all things." (Moroni 10:5). Remember the God of the loaves and fishes cares about your life mission and He will guide you to it if you will but listen through the Spirit. He will guide you to all truth and tell you on what side of the boat to cast your nets. Just like the nerve connections between your gut and your brain, there is a line to connect us with the Infinite and with a world beyond our world. We can tap into the collective wisdom of the ages if we just plug into the Spirit. Do all you can to seek the Spirit and you will feel in your mind and your heart that you have found your unique life mission.

So please, avoid an ulcer, trust your gut, and plug into the Spirit that will lead you to a life that is much better than anything you could imagine for yourself.

*LDS Footnote: Think of the implications of being able to "feel" the Spirit based on what we eat or don't eat according to the Word of Wisdom. I believe there was much more revealed when our prophets counseled us to eat well than just avoiding addictive substances, but we'll save that for another day.

Chapter 14
Surround Yourself with Greatness

"If I have seen further it is by standing on the shoulders of giants."

- Isaac Newton

E very April in Philadelphia, thousands of athletes from all over the world gather for what I believe to be one of the most amazing events on earth: The Penn Relay Carnival. Track athletes as young as middle school get to run and compete on the same track as Olympians. I had the opportunity to run in the Penn Relays twice during high school. I remember my junior year seeing Michael Johnson, Marion Jones, Maurice Greene (the fastest humans on the planet at that time), and other amazing athletes running on the same track as me. I remember thinking that I was in the presence of greatness. After I had seen the USA 4X100m and 4X400m relay team demolish the rest of the teams (from Scotland, Jamaica, Germany, etc.), I was totally on fire. I wanted to put my spikes on and turn up the gas like I never had before. I wanted to be as fast as Michael Johnson and at that moment, I actually believed that I could reach his level at some point! After that, I went on to become the captain of the track team at my high school as well as my collegiate team. I broke a seventeen-year-standing high school record as well as many collegiate records in my small college, and I even became a collegiate all-American. I would never have believed this was possible if I hadn't tasted the nectar of greatness at the Penn Relays.

I don't share this to brag about the glory days, but to show that when we surround ourselves with greatness, it rubs off on us. We are strengthened by the greatness around us. A little piece of Michael Johnson rubbed off on me and gave me the vision to do something I would never have imagined. The same is true for you. Don't surround yourself with people who drag you down and don't believe in you. Hanging around constant criticism and negativity will *never* help you find your life mission. This type of person will not believe in you or even that you have a mission in life. They will probably just say that having a calling in life is a bunch of hogwash. Don't spend your time with people like this. Why would you? Consider this profound statement by Gordon B. Hinckley about the influence of negative people around us:

> Sir Walter Scott was a trouble to all his teachers and so was Lord Byron. Thomas Edison, as everyone knows, was considered a dullard in school. Pestalozzi, who later became Italy's foremost educator, was regarded as wild and foolish by his school authorities. Oliver Goldsmith was considered almost an imbecile. The Duke of Wellington failed in many of his classes. Among famous writers, Burns, Balzac, Boccaccio, and Dumas made poor academic records. Flaubert, who went on to become France's most impeccable writer, found it extremely difficult to learn to read. Thomas Aquinas, who had the finest scholastic mind of all Catholic

thinkers, was actually dubbed "the dumb ox" at school. Linnaeus and Volta did badly in their studies. Newton was last in his class. Sheridan, the English playwright, wasn't able to stay in one school more than a year. All of this seems to say to me that each of these men, every one of whom later became great, might have done much better in his studies had he received less of criticism and more of encouragement. (Gordon B. Hinckley, Let Not Your Heart Be Troubled, BYU Speeches Oct. 29, 1974.)

What if they had surrounded themselves with great instructors, inspiring peers, and edifying mentors? These heroes in history may have even become greater than they already were! As you seek to find your mission in life, you must surround yourself with the best and the brightest, with those who will lift you up, with people who will inspire you to be your best self, to reach past the low hanging fruit for the great potential joy of the fruits hanging higher. Anyone can reach them if they can only observe it. Sometimes we just need to watch someone else succeed to believe that it is possible for us to do the same.

Even if you have no idea what you want to be or do, spend time with people who *do* know their purpose and calling in life and who are *living* their purpose. It will rub off on you. Find a lot of these great people in a lot of different areas (remember what I mentioned about trying on lots of hats.) If you can't find anyone, go watch five TED talks, go to the Olympics, or stop into the office hours of a super sharp professor and just chat. Take a millionaire to lunch (there are a lot who are willing to be taken to lunch) and pick their brain about how they got there. Go to some networking events and meet entrepreneurs who are starting businesses or whose businesses are already booming. Go to a live performance where you can witness the best performers in the world. Ask your parents who their heroes are. Look at the NYT best-seller list and email or tweet every single one of the authors. (You will probably hear back from at least one. I just tweeted a best-selling author last week, and she personally retweeted my tweet!). Just being with someone who is the embodiment of greatness in their own way can bring the spirit of greatness into your heart. And if you are listening, you might just hear your spirit tell you what *you* are to become and what *you* are to do. Remember though, when you are with people who are passionate about what they do, you may catch the bug of what *they* are passionate about and think that this is your calling because *they* are so passionate about it. If that truly is your passion, then GREAT! If not, keep moving forward. How do you know? Remember what I said about finding flow. If you skimmed that chapter, go back and read it now. And trust your gut, remember?

There is an interesting body of research in the world of positive psychology about what are called mirror neurons. These mirror neurons are the reason a yawn spreads in a meeting. Positive psychologist Shawn Achor teaches about this in his trainings and on his viral TED talk. Mirror neurons are "specialized brain cells that can actually sense and then mimic the feelings, actions, and physical sensations of another person." (Shawn Achor, *The Happiness Advantage,* p. 203-204). So when we observe another person get a painful papercut when carelessly licking an envelope, even though we aren't the one with a bleeding tongue, the same set of neurons that are associated with "papercut on tongue" pain light up in our brain just as well as the careless licker. I'm not trying to get you to change your major to neuroscience. I'm just trying to show you that our mirror neurons will actually mimic in our brains what we are observing in others. With this in mind, who would want to spend time with a person who complains all day and moans about how much they hate their life, someone who is completely apathetic, someone who is constantly negative about everything around them (including you), or someone who never smiles or laughs or plays or relaxes? Over time, these things will *literally* rub off on you through your mirror neurons.

So find amazing people. The type of giants that Isaac Newton learned from and the heroes of the heroes. Spend time with life's Olympians and it will rub off on you. You'll be a better person because of it. And there will be a ripple effect of positivity and greatness that doesn't stop at you, but that spreads to thousands of other people who you don't even know.

Surround yourself with greatness, and you'll know what to do with your life.

Chapter 15
Use the Happiness Advantage

"I have begun to be somewhat merry because I have been told that that is good for one's health."

- Voltaire

I had just eaten lunch at the campus cafeteria at Southern Virginia University when I got a call (on a landline phone) from the school post office. The receptionist said in a very heavy southern Virginia accent, "You gotta a big white envelope here that you might want to come pick up." It was my mission call. I had been waiting for weeks for this. I ran down to the post office as fast as my track star feet could carry me and grabbed the envelope. This was a moment I had been waiting for all my life. Inside this envelope awaited an assignment from a prophet of God that could take me anywhere on Earth! I had an a capella concert to sing in that night and a philosophy final the next morning at 7:00 am to prepare for. I didn't have time to try to contact all my family and friends that night before my concert and my last final exam as a freshman. I decided to wait. I slipped my mission call into my desk drawer with a huge smile on my face and a sense of life-satisfaction that I had never experienced in my whole life. I studied for a few hours, sang my little heart out in the concert and then studied a little more. As I studied, it was as if I had an added ability to memorize all these philosophical proofs from Plato to Anselm to Aquinas to Aristotle. It was as if my brain were on fire! I don't know if I had ever had as good of a study session as I did that night. I went to bed with excitement in my heart and philosophy in my mind. I woke up early the next morning to make it to my 7:00 am philosophy final. My brain recalled perfectly every single one of the theorems and proofs and concepts of each and every philosopher the entire semester as if it were a game. I aced my final and left the room with a big smile on my face. I was one happy nineteen-year-old.

The point of this story isn't to brag about my ability to memorize philosophical proofs but to point out that my brain was aided by the fact that I was so happy. I believe I actually got a better grade on my final because of the incredible amount of positive emotion I was experiencing. I also believe that if I would have waited until after my philosophy final was over to soak in the happiness of the fact that I had received my mission call (because I hadn't even opened it yet), I would have gotten a less than optimal score. This cognitive effect is what positive psychologists call "the happiness advantage."

One of the most impressive evangelists of the happiness advantage is Shawn Achor, a young Harvard professor who has written a book about this phenomenon. Here's Shawn:

> New research in psychology and neuroscience shows that . . . we become more successful when we are happier and more positive. For example, doctors put in a positive mood before making a diagnosis show almost three times more intelligence and creativity than doctors in a neutral state, and they make accurate diagnoses 19 percent faster. Optimistic salespeople outsell their counterparts by 56 percent. Students primed to feel happy before taking math achievement tests far outperform their neutral peers. *It turns out that our brains are literally hardwired to perform at their best not when they are negative or even neutral, but when they are positive* (*The Happiness Advantage*, p. 15).

My whole life, I have been taught the exact opposite: wait until you are successful, then be happy.

Once I graduate, then I can be happy.

Once I get into grad school, then I can be happy.

Once I find a girlfriend (or boyfriend), then I'll be happy.

As soon as I finish my book, then I can be happy.

As soon as I get that great job, then I can be happy.

Once I finish my paper, then I will be happy.

Once I'm done with my project, then I can be happy.

I have always thought this way until I read about the happiness advantage. The extra creativity, cognitive ability and innovation that we need to accomplish these things and to be successful could be acquired if we allow ourselves to be happy before we hit the milestones. Positive emotion may very well be the added edge we need to push ourselves to the top!

It's not just theoretical or hypothetical either; it's actually biological. Happiness gives us a real-life chemical edge. How does it do this? Here is Shawn again (*The Happiness Advantage*, p. 44):

> Positive emotions flood our brains with dopamine and serotonin, chemicals that not only make us feel good but dial up the learning centers of our brains to higher levels. They help us organize new information, keep that information in the brain longer, and retrieve it faster later on. And they enable us to make and sustain more neural connections, which allows us to think more quickly and creatively, become more skilled at complex analysis and problem-solving, and see and invent new ways of doing things.

This happiness advantage will accelerate your brain as you are trying to figure out your mission in life. So don't just think that you can only be happy once you have figured out what to do with your life. Or that you will only be able to really relax once you are on the right track. This thinking is actually counterproductive. What makes you happy right now? What brings a smile to your face? Where do you feel like you can just play and relax? What activities make you glad to be alive? How often do you laugh? How often do you play? How much everyday happiness do you experience? If it's not a lot, you should create more. Everyday happiness creates the positive emotion you need to give you the advantage.

Create more positive emotion in your life, and you will be given the happiness advantage to push you toward the discovery of your personal mission. And once you discover your mission, use the happiness advantage to make you even more effective and productive in accomplishing your life mission!

Be happy now. Don't wait until you have everything figured out. Being happy now will give you the happiness advantage, propelling you toward your greatest potential in living your mission.

Chapter 16
Ask God, Not Siri.

"And their wisdom shall be great, and their understanding reach to heaven; and before them the wisdom of the wise shall perish, and the understanding of the prudent shall come to naught. For by my Spirit will I enlighten them, and by my power will I make known unto them the secrets of my will--yea, even those things which eye has not seen, nor ear heard, nor yet entered into the heart of man."

- D&C 76:9-10

Karen Hepworth changed my life forever. She probably doesn't even remember who I am now, but I remember her. Why? Because I discovered my life mission while sitting in an ordinary room in an ordinary class with an *extraordinary teacher.* I was taking an ordinary class (Doctrines of the Gospel), and we were just talking about an ordinary subject: the purpose of life on Earth. She began the class by telling the story of Elder Russell M. Nelson—the heart surgeon turned apostle. She shared a fact about him that I will never forget. Elder Nelson believes that he had a very specific life mission, and that mission was to become one of the best heart surgeons in the world so that he could save the life of a prophet of God. And he did just that. President Spencer W. Kimball's life was saved by Russell M. Nelson precisely because he was one of the greatest heart surgeons on earth. He was on the team that created the first heart-lung machine, which made the first open-heart surgery possible in 1951. She told of how he had a specific mission and that he accomplished it. Then she asked the class, "What is your purpose on Earth? Not just the purpose of coming to this life in general, but *your* specific purpose." And she gave us ten minutes to just think and write. I experienced something similar to what Joseph Smith said, "When you feel pure intelligence flowing into you, it may give you sudden strokes of ideas." (*TPJS*, sel. Joseph Fielding Smith [1976], 151.) It was as if all the stars aligned in my life up to this point and I knew my personal purpose in life. I didn't know *how* to accomplish it, but it became very clear to me what it was (you can find my personal life mission printed in the beginning of this book).

This one class changed my life forever because I trusted that God could tell me, through the Spirit what my unique life mission was, and He did. Did He tell me how to accomplish that mission? Nope. He just sent a personalized message to let me know why I'm here. Since then, I have strived to align all I do with that purpose.

We are super accustomed to finding instant answers because of very well programmed search algorithms. For example:

"tax forms for paying contractors"

"when is Easter this year?"

"how to build an iPhone app"

"how to remove zits in Photoshop"

"top ranked universities"

"best company to work for"

"how to reduce stress at family gatherings"

"how much do lawyers make?"

"movie times in Provo, UT"

"what does the fox say?"

"how many people live in India?"

"sushi restaurant near me"

"who are the presidential candidates?"

"how long does it take to become a PA?"

Every single one of these answers will be given to you in less than a second (unless you are on dial-up) by asking any search engine like Siri or Google. This is amazing! I love the convenience, and I think in terms of Googling. I'm a bit biased because I worked as a website search engine optimizer for a few years, but the general zeitgeist of the day is that if we have a question, we can find an answer instantaneously with a tap of a finger on our smart device. What happens when we ask Siri the question:

"What is my personal life mission?"

or

"What is my purpose in this life?"

or

"What is my mission in life?"

That kind of answer doesn't come instantly from a search algorithm robot. It's an answer that requires substance and personalization that no search engine (no matter how many cookies you have on your browser) can provide. This kind of personalized answer can only come from someone who knows you well— someone who knows you even better than you know yourself.

God is the ultimate source of light and truth, and if you seek Him, He will help you find the right pathway toward your personal life mission. He has promised this, "If thou shalt ask, thou shalt receive revelation upon revelation, knowledge upon knowledge, that thou mayest know the mysteries and peaceable things—that which bringeth joy, that which bringeth life eternal." (D&C 42:61). I believe that there is nothing that will bring you more lasting joy than to know your personal life mission. That is something that God wants to help you find, and He has promised that He will help you find it if you seek Him, if you ask, and if you listen.

Remember to seek for God as you seek for your personal life mission. Ask God. He will help you. He may do it in a very ordinary circumstance, but He will do it if you are listening. When you ask

God instead of Google, it will take longer, but if you're listening, you'll get a foundational answer that will guide you the rest of your life.

Author's Note on patriarchal blessings: A lot of you are probably thinking, "wait a minute, don't we already have a personalized message from the Lord about our life in our patriarchal blessing?" The answer is yes. You do. Patriarchal blessings are a wonderful guide in your life that can provide principles to help you your whole life! We believe that these blessings are inspired of God, like a light to guide you along the pathway. Don't disregard your patriarchal blessing in your quest to find your life mission. My life mission is perfectly in line with my patriarchal blessing. I also know many people who get very discouraged and even feel stuck because their blessing paints a picture of a life that does not reflect what they want to become. It also may not reflect what they *want* to do. Some almost feel forced into a pathway they wouldn't otherwise choose with their natural capabilities or God-given gifts. If you feel this way, I would counsel you to remember that the entire plan of salvation is based on the principle of *agency*. God will never force you to do anything. The purpose of this life is to learn how to use our agency well. What God *does* want is for us to use the atonement to purify our desires so that we will actually *want* to choose to become like Him. I also believe that your life mission is unique to *you* and because of this, it will differ like a thumbprint differs. Every thumbprint is unique. Your life mission is not a cookie cutter, one-size-fits-all type of thing. It is personal and unique, and it is very important. I believe that what matters most to God isn't the tasks and activities that your life mission will involve, but how your unique life mission will carve out your character and what it will make you become. God levels the playing field by allowing us all to use our agency to develop our unique character. Therefore, either some life missions would be more important than others (how could you top saving the life of a prophet?), and there is much less room for diversity in the kingdom of God. *Or* all of us have a unique life mission within the kingdom of God, and we get to use that personalized journey to carve out our character and our character is what God really cares about. The latter is what I believe with all my soul. And no matter how many patriarchal blessings have been given, we should all still seek for the unique diversity within our soul. That diversity is the very thing that makes God's kingdom so heavenly. Please don't misunderstand my value of patriarchal blessings. I only bring this up because of the people I have spoken to who have real concerns about why their patriarchal blessing seems very generic and unspecific. This is my answer to those people.

Chapter 17
Have a Chat with Death

"The fear of death follows from the fear of life. A man who lives fully is prepared to die at any time." -Mark Twain

I remember freezing my buns off standing in a line outside the conference center in Salt Lake City. There were over forty-thousand others that night braving the 18 degree° Fahrenheit weather and 17 mph winds. I felt like I was going to get hypothermia, and I was wearing thermal underwear and two coats. I have no idea how the young women in skirts ever survived. A similar crowd would come the next night in similar arctic weather. We were all there because of one man: Gordon Bitner Hinckley. He passed away on January 27, 2008, and we were at his public viewing. He was one of my heroes. He signed my mission call. He was a prophet of God and a true giant among men. His passing had an effect on millions of people. He will be remembered for generations to come. When I think of the type of person I want to become, I think of Gordon B. Hinckley. Going to his viewing solidified this. I don't want to be the prophet of the Church, but I do want to have a positive impact on many people. I am a better person because of Gordon B. Hinckley, and his life made me want to live my life to the fullest.

Thinking about death clarifies your life. When you go to someone's funeral, you get to reflect on the impact that a person had in life, the good things they did and the person they became. You also get a very clear demonstration that this life has an end. When you see this clearly, even when you are mourning the loss of someone you loved, it helps you to take a step back and look at yourself (like we mentioned in the first chapter). You can really look at where you are, where you want to be, and what course corrections you might need to make. Joseph B. Wirthlin talked about this in a speech he gave shortly before he passed away:

> Examine your life. Determine where you are and what you need to do to be the kind of person you want to be. Create inspiring, noble, and righteous goals that fire your imagination and create excitement in your heart. And then keep your eye on them. Work consistently towards achieving them. (Joseph B. Wirthlin, *Life Lessons Learned*, General Conference, April 2007)

Going to a funeral or a cemetery allows us to have a little chat with death without dying. We are given a vicarious glimpse of the end without having to see our own end. This glimpse can be very useful for a few different reasons. First, it can help us to act because we are reminded that we don't live forever. You'll read more about the real benefits of just acting in the next chapter. Second, it can be very inspirational to go to funerals because, even though funeral speeches are often a bit hyperbolic in nature, people highlight all the greatest accomplishments of the one who passed away. This exaggerated amazingness placed in our laps from the pulpit can inspire us to reach higher. And though the things that are said may be a bit unrealistic (or at least somewhat exaggerated), we naturally feel great reverence and respect when someone dies. This respect for the dead can help us to raise our sights to a higher ideal. I'm not saying you should set your goals and ideals to an unrealistic standard, but going to a funeral can be an incredible way to be inspired to be your highest self. And as you become more in touch with your highest self, you will become more and more clear about what your personal life mission is.

Going to a funeral can help you create a bucket list (we will talk about this in chapter 20). There is a new movement that was started in New Orleans by a woman named Candy Chang. One of her dear friends died, and it affected her so much that she decided to dedicate her next big project to this friend. She found an old abandoned house that was in a place with a lot of foot traffic, and she converted it into something inspiring. She converted the most prominent wall into a large chalkboard with large painted words "BEFORE I DIE . . . " and then painted around a hundred slots that say in smaller text: "Before I die, I want to_____" People started filling in the blanks with their hopes and dreams. This one board was then created into a movement. Her *Before I Die* wall has been created now in over 1,000 cities in over 70 countries all over the world.

Discovering your life mission has a lot to do with figuring out what you want to do before you die. As you seek to discover your life mission, take some time to contemplate death so that you can fully live.

Chapter 18
Think NIKE and Seize the Day

"Carpe Diem" - Horace

I was almost Joseph Smith. Well, sort of. The summer before my junior year of high school I was approached by a middle-aged man at church. He came up to me with a smile on his face, introduced himself and asked me, "Do you want to be in a movie?" I said, "Sure, what do you mean?" He then told me, "I'm the writer of the newest film about the restoration, and you have the look we want for Joseph Smith. Will you come try out?" I had absolutely no acting background, but I thought it sounded fun, so I said yes. After a few call backs and an acting coach, they said they wanted me to be Joseph Smith, but that I had to be approved by the First Presidency. A few months later, the motion picture studio came back with a decision that went something like this, "The First Presidency didn't want you because you look too old to them, but we still want you to be in the movie as Joseph's brother Hyrum." I was never expecting to be Joseph in the first place, so I wasn't really let down by their decision, and I thought it was cool that I could still be in the movie. So I asked them what it required of me to be Hyrum. They then told me that I would need to come out for quite a few shoots during fall, winter, and then more in the summer and that I would likely need to be homeschooled because I would miss so much school for the shooting. They gave me the dates. I looked at my calendar, and I didn't care as much about the school part, but I did care about the fact that I would be giving up my track career. After about a week of thinking and praying about it, I declined the offer. I'm really glad that I chose track. However, for years I wondered what could have come of it if I would have been Hyrum. On my mission, especially, I had a hard time because I was showing all my investigators the video

I had the opportunity to be a part of. I'll never know what would have happened if I chose to be Hyrum, and that will kind of haunt me.

As humans, we are pretty good at finding the silver lining on the cloud of *bad* decisions we make. We have less regret on something we actually did (or at least we are better at overcoming it). However, it is even harder for us to look back on an opportunity we *didn't* take. The regret for missed opportunities is much more difficult to overcome than the regret for an opportunity we took that turned bad. Harvard professor Dan Gilbert talks about this in his book *Stumbling on Happiness*:

> Indeed, in the long run, people of every age and in every walk of life seem to regret not having done things much more than they regret things they did, which is why the most popular regrets include not going to college, not grasping profitable business opportunities, and not spending enough time with family and friends.

Want to know the things that people regret most? A study by Neal Roese, a professor at Kellogg School of Management, agrees with Dan Gilbert. In a meta-analysis, (basically a mega study of studies) they found the top five things that were related to the greatest levels of regret for people:

1. Education
2. Career
3. Romance
4. Parenting
5. Self

Education was by far the winner in this category and Roese says that it is because education breeds so much opportunity (Roese, Neal

J. (2005). *If only. How to turn regret into opportunity*. New York: Broadway Books).

So why does this matter in a book about determining and living your life mission? After you have discovered your life mission, you may not find the nexus point (see the chapter about finding the nexus point) until after you have taken a lot different opportunities. When an opportunity comes up, you may find that you need to follow what Nike says and just do it. Carpe diem! Seize the day! Go for it! Take the bull by the horns! Do you remember what I said in the chapter about trying on lots of hats? You'll have much less regret if you just jump on the great opportunities that are given to you than if you avoid taking risks and never take the opportunities in front of you. I love what former Vice President Dick Cheney said at a BYU commencement address in 2007:

> Many of you will leave BYU today with definite plans of your own. And setting a plan for your life can be a good thing. It keeps you focused on the future and gives you a standard for measuring your progress. Yet I would guess that ten years from now many of you will find yourselves following a very different course—all because of an opportunity that came out of the blue. Be on the watch for those certain moments and certain people that come along and point you in a new direction . . . For all the plans we make in life, sometimes life has other plans for us.

Don't be afraid to commit to an opportunity that pops up out of nowhere. Just do it. You may regret it later, but you won't regret it as much as contemplating what might have come of it after you don't take that opportunity. Sometimes committing to something is just what we need to see that it is right. We must commit, move, and act when we are given an opportunity. As Goethe has said:

Until one is committed, there is hesitancy, the chance to draw back . . . Concerning all acts of initiative (and creation), there is one elementary truth the ignorance of which kills countless ideas and splendid plans: that the moment one definitely commits oneself, then Providence moves too. All sorts of things occur to help one that would never otherwise have occurred. A whole stream of events issues from the decision, raising in one's favor all manner of unforeseen incidents, meetings and material assistance which no man could have dreamed would have come his way. Whatever you can do or dream you can, begin it. Boldness has genius, power and magic in it. Begin it now.

Don't be afraid to move and commit to an opportunity you are given. Go for it. Just do it. Things will work out as you move ahead with confidence and you won't ever have to worry about the regret of not taking that opportunity. Trust your gut, and go for it.

Chapter 19
Drop Everything and Go to Your Happy Place

"If people sat outside and looked at the stars each night, I'll bet they'd live a lot differently." - Calvin (Calvin and Hobbes)

It was 9:00 pm and the sun was just setting when I got a text from my buddy Derrick:

"Wanna go shoot the Perseids?" (long exposure photography of a meteor shower)

"Yes. Where?"

"Arches National Park."

"Wait. When?"

"Right now."

"Um, okay. Let's do it."

We lived in Provo, and it took us three hours to get there. By the time we arrived, it was one in the morning. We ended up shooting at a cloudy sky, but Derrick, our friend Anna, and I slept under a gigantic monolith called "balancing rock." I could almost feel the gravity of the towering stone pulling us closer to it. It was as if it was alive. It was uncomfortable sleeping on a bunch of rocks with the possibility of snakes, lizards or scorpions wandering in to get warm from our body heat. Despite these discomforts, it was one of the most memorable nights of my life because I left my vain repetition of daily life to be inspired by something, and I was. And it wasn't even the meteor shower, it was this huge rock that was barely visible. On our way back, I remember we had an amazing conversation about what we are doing in life. At that point, I had already discovered what my life mission was, but we were brainstorming how to make it happen. We talked of world travel mixed with photography, videography, and interviewing people from all different cultures about what makes them happy. We almost started a new organization right there in the car! It was a beautiful night of dreaming big and progressing toward my purpose in life because I went to my happy place with those who believed in me. I could have stayed home and slept in a comfortable bed, but I'm so glad I didn't.

You need a happy place. A place to recharge the batteries of your soul. This could happen for different people in different places, but everyone has at least one.

My happy place has been found in many places doing many different things. In addition to the one above, I have found it when I was running half-clothed through a water-filled slot canyon in southern Utah. I have found it nearly getting hypothermia while shooting a long-exposure time-lapse of a frozen waterfall at 2:00 am. I have found it when singing for a Franciscan monk in an ancient church in Jerusalem. I have found it in my bedroom on my knees. I have found it while running a seven-mile night leg of a two-hundred-mile relay in the middle of a Californian desert with nothing to light my path but the stars and a headlamp. And I have found it in the celestial room of the temple. I have found it while writing in my journal on a plane ride over the Atlantic. I have found it praying next to my Orthodox Jewish rabbi friend at the Western Wall in Jerusalem. I always find it early in the morning walking along a Californian beach.

Every time I plug into my happy place, I remember myself. I remember why I'm here. I remember what I'm doing here. I am able to reach into the wisdom within me. Not only am I able to remember what I am supposed to be doing, but I see clearly all the things I spend so much of my time doing that don't matter in the long run. It gives me perspective.

The big picture is mine again.

Finding your happy place can really help when you are seeking to discover and solidify your life mission because it helps you clear the air. Even anticipation of going to your happy place can help increase positive emotion and improve your performance no matter at what stage you are.

When you are trying to discover your mission in life, go to your happy place. Doing so will help you gain an added measure of perspective as you move forward with commitment to accomplish your dream. It will also inoculate you against making fast and easy decisions to do something just for the money or social pressure.

Don't forget to go to your happy place as you decide how to accomplish your life mission. It will fire the flames within you and push you forward on your way.

Chapter 20
Create a BE Bucket List

"Many of the things you can count, don't count. Many of the things you can't count, really count." - *Albert Einstein*

I have a bucket list. Some of the things on my bucket list include jumping into a large body of water with all my clothes on, downhill skiing in a gorilla suit, going to Rome before I turn 30, going on a honeymoon to the Holy Land with my wife, and many others. Just like me, I think people often think about life in terms of what we want to *do*. We create long lists of things to do before we "kick the bucket." Some things I have seen on many bucket lists include:

Go skydiving.

Hike the Appalachian Trail.

Run a marathon.

Backpack across Europe.

Swim with dolphins.

Go on an Alaskan cruise.

Ride an elephant in Thailand.

Earn a doctorate degree.

Go to the great pyramids of Egypt.

Buy a house.

Make a million dollars in one year.

Write a book.

Learn a foreign language.

These all sound amazing! I'm really not against creating a list that motivates you and animates the fire of life in your heart. Actually, I think God wants us to do things that fill our hearts with hope and help us to look forward to the future. Everyone should strive for happiness and fulfillment in their lives.

Personally, I believe the happiest and most fulfilled people on this earth are those who are constantly working on a different kind of bucket list. And that happiness and fulfillment did not come because they BASE jumped off the Burj Khalifa in Dubai (though this would be a way cool thing to tell your friends). It also didn't come because they hiked a mountain and took a selfie with some Tibetan monks.

I believe the ultimate bucket list would have less to do with what we are doing and more to do with what we are becoming. Here is my idea of the ultimate life bucket list:

Become filled with love for everyone, even my enemies.

Become a compassionate person.

Become a good listener.

Become a meek and humble person.

Become a person of absolute confidence.

Become a person filled with light and truth.

Become someone who loves learning.

Become a master teacher.

Become a servant to all.

Become patient.

Become trustworthy.

Become someone who hungers and thirsts after righteousness.

Become merciful and develop a forgiving heart.

Become pure in heart.

Become a peacemaker.

Become like Jesus.

This list is the ultimate list because it challenges us not just to *do* something, but to *become* something more—to become like Jesus. I believe Jesus Christ was and is the most happy and fulfilled person not because of what He has checked off a bucket list of accomplishments (or cool things to post on Facebook or Twitter), but because of what He has become. And I believe that we will not find the greatest fulfillment in life from posting selfies from the Great Wall of China or any number of cool accomplishments, but by what we are becoming.

It's like Dieter F. Uchtdorf said, quoting Albert Einstein:

"Many of the things you can count, do not count. Many of the things you cannot count, really do count."

God's plan of salvation is perfect for everyone precisely because it asks us not to *do* something great, but to *become* someone great. It levels the playing field. Becoming patient weighs equally on God's scale whether you are an Olympic hurdler or a leper in a wheelchair. Becoming pure in heart weighs equally on God's scale whether you are a fifty-five--year--old mother of ten kids or a fifty-five--year--old woman who never married. Becoming merciful weighs equally on God's scale whether you have three advanced degrees from Ivy League universities, or you never finished high school. Ultimately, God will see not what we have *done*, but what we have *become*, and this list of becoming more Christlike is the ultimate bucket list, no matter your age, race, vocation, location, or relationship status. Jesus challenged us to become more when He said, "Therefore, what manner of men ought ye to be? Verily I say unto you, *even as I am*" (3 Nephi 27:27; italics added).

And Ezra Taft Benson added this, "Walking in His way is the greatest achievement of life. That man or woman is most truly successful whose life most closely parallels that of the Master." (Ezra Taft Benson, Teachings of Presidents of the Church: Ezra Taft Benson, (2014), 296–306).

As you discover your unique life mission, don't hesitate to create your bucket list of things you want to do or see or accomplish in your life. Doing this really can inspire you. Just remember that as you accomplish and do, what you are *becoming* matters most of all. And when you look at life through this lens, you will become most clear on what your life mission is and why it matters.

In the end, your life mission is all about what you are becoming. No matter what you end up doing in accomplishing your life mission, what you are becoming because of this is what will have the most impact on you in this life and the next.

Here's to your journey of becoming.

Chapter 21
Find The NEXUS Point

"The fox knows many things, but the hedgehog knows one big thing." - Archilochus

What if you already know what your life mission is? First of all, congratulations! Celebrate that achievement! There are so many who go their whole life without reaching that point. If you still haven't figured it out by now, keep looking. And reading this chapter will give you a competitive edge as you do seek.

Can you discover your personal life mission without knowing *how* to accomplish it? YES. So many people feel that they know what their mission is in life, but they have no idea how to do something related to this dream that will be in any way sustainable for them or their family. I know some people who have actually chosen to work in another field (that is not their calling in life) so that they can, in their spare time, do something that *is* related to their calling. I call these people avocational dreamers. They have a vocation, but what they really dream of is their avocation—the thing that they actually *enjoy* doing in their free time after coming home from their full-time vocation.

You may find yourself in this position. If this is the case, I am not telling you that you are bad for doing this. It says a lot about your character that you would work hard, even when you don't like what you do. However, consider your primary line of work and see where it falls on the following scale from University of Pennsylvania's positive psychology site www.authentichappiness.org:

Job: Something that you don't like doing, but you do because if you didn't, you wouldn't be able to make ends meet. If there were any way to get out of it, you would. Time off is what you look forward to. There is no forward movement or hope of progress. There is a ceiling that you will never be able to rise above no matter how long you work at this job and no matter how skilled you are. It just fills the role of paying bills, period.

Career: Unlike a job, a career has the potential to get you where you want to be. It fills the bill-paying role and also has the hope of progressing onto what you really want. You actually enjoy some aspects of the job part, and you know that it is going to move you forward toward what you really want and love. It could be a really important part of helping you get to the place of what you are really passionate about in life.

Calling: Not only does this pay the bills, but it is what you would choose to do if you could do anything. You don't like leaving work because you love it. You feel that what you are doing is making the world a better place. Even if you didn't make money from it, you would desire to do it. You feel satisfied at the end of every day and look forward to the start of every day. The work you do is hard, but you love it. You wake up excited most mornings instead of dreading your alarm clock each day.

Does your line of work feel more like a job, career, or calling? The goal of this chapter (and this book) is not only to help you find your mission in life but to *live your mission*. But how can you do this if you have to pay the bills by doing something that feels like a job? How can you not get stuck feeling like you are just working day in and day out doing something that you would try to get out of if you could?

I think it has everything to do with finding the nexus point in what Jim Collins (see more in his amazing book *Good To Great)* calls the Hedgehog Concept. What is that? It is when three crucial factors come together. Here are the factors:

    1. Natural Passion - you feel it is your calling in life, you love it.

    2. Natural ability - you could possibly become the best in the world at it.

    3. Economic engine - a need exists or can be innovated for the thing you are doing.

The magic begins when all three of these exist together. Jim Collins calls it the Hedgehog Concept based on the famous essay "The Hedgehog and the Fox" by Isaiah Berlin. When we can be more like the hedgehog (having found the nexus point between the three factors above) and less like the fox (jumping from one job to the next, or being flung from career to career), we will be able to truly flourish.

To have a fully developed Hedgehog Concept, you need all three factors. If you only make a lot of money doing things at which you could never be the best, you will only build a successful career, not a fulfilling calling. If you become the best at something, you won't stay that way for long if you don't have the natural and intrinsic passion for what you are doing. And lastly, you can have all the passion in the world, but if you can't become great at it, or it doesn't make any economic sense (and there is no need for it), then you may have a lot of fun doing it (and even find meaning in it), but it will never be sustainable. The dream will die soon after it has been born.

I believe there is a way to find the nexus point where we are actually living the Hedgehog Concept. It's not one perfect note on the scale, but three perfect notes to create an unbreakable harmony. When all three are played together, you can feel it in your bones.

When you find the nexus point, others hear the harmony within you and see the fire in your eyes. You move forward with a certainty and confidence that is contagious. When people are around you, they want to know why you seem so happy.

You may not reach this perfect harmony at first, but I believe it is something that is worth working toward. You might find yourself in the "career" category for a while before you find a way to join all three of the factors together to find the nexus point.

James Allen described people who have found the nexus point in his essay called "Visions and Ideals." The only way that they become so influential is not because they are dreamers, but because they are dreamers who have found that perfect harmony, and who make it happen. Here are his wise words:

> The dreamers are the saviours of the world. As the visible world is sustained by the invisible, so men, through all their trials and sins and sordid vocations, are nourished by the beautiful visions of their solitary dreamers. Composer, sculptor, painter, poet, prophet, sage, these are the makers of the after-world, the architects of heaven. The world is beautiful because they have lived; without them, laboring humanity would perish. Cherish your visions; cherish your ideals; cherish the music that stirs in your heart, the beauty that forms in your mind, the loveliness that drapes your purest thoughts, for out of them will grow all delightful conditions, all heavenly environment; of these, if you but remain true to them, your world will at last be built (*As a Man Thinketh*, from the chapter "Visions and Ideals").

Your world awaits you. As you dedicate yourself to discovering and living your personal mission in life, your heaven will begin to be built. Everything you do to live your mission will become a part of the makeup of your soul—something that will go with you into the next life. As you lay bricks in this life of the person you are becoming, the same bricks are being used to build your heavenly estate. Build wisely. Don't build structures here that you don't want to have to take down later. Build your life around what you desire to become. If you are okay with settling for less than your full potential in this life, that is what will be given to you here *and in the next life*. But if you push yourself to reach for the higher hanging fruits in this life, the same fruits will be yours in the hereafter. Be deliberate in the architecture of your own personal heaven, because *you* are the one who is building it. Find the nexus point and live your mission for this life and forever.

Appendix A - Supporting Books

My life has been changed by the books that I have read and the people who surround me. This book has largely been influenced by other books that I have read. You need to constantly be digesting helpful and inspiring content and you'll have the resources you need to find your mission and live it every day of your life. These books have helped me find and live my mission and I hope they can help you as well.

How Will You Measure Your Life - Clayton Christensen

The Element - Ken Robinson

The Success Principles - Jack Canfield

The Life of Pi - Yan Martel

Leadership and Self Deception - Arbinger Institute

The Paradox of Choice - Barry Schwartz

The How of Happiness - Sonja Lyubomirski

The Happiness Advantage - Shawn Achor

Flourish - Martin Seligman

The Greatest Salesman in the World - Og Mandino

The Great Divorce - C.S. Lewis

As a Man Thinketh - James Allen

Winning With People - John C. Maxwell

10 Great Souls I want to Meet in Heaven - S. Michael Wilcox

Hearing the Voice of the Lord - Gerald Lund

The Continuous Atonement - Brad Wilcox

Pure in Heart - Dallin H. Oaks

Good to Great - Jim Collins

The Alchemist - Paulo Coelho

Appendix B - Bonus Chapter
Step Outside Your Cave
and Take a Look

"The unexamined life is not worth living." - Plato

Author's Note: This chapter got thrown out of the 21 principles because it wasn't the best, but I wanted to include it in the book still so it is a bonus for what it is worth. If you can take something from this, great. Though there may be a nugget or two from this chapter, I like the other chapters better.

If we never take the time just to step back from the seventeen things to get done this week at the office, the three papers to write, two midterm exams to study for, and the GRE test to prepare for, routine can take over our lives. If we allow this to happen, we may look back after twenty years of routine to find that we haven't been singing the song we came here to sing.

Step back for a day or a week (or a year) to explore who you are. Take a good look at it *outside* the context of your job, your major, or the way you make money to pay your bills and seriously consider the God-given gifts inside of you.

When I was at BYU, I was constantly lost in the minutia of every day until I heard a forum speech by Robert C. Oaks that helped me to step back. He said that even though it is important to study the things that will help you in your career, it is *even more important* to discover, while you are here, *who you are in God's plan.*

One of the best nuggets of western literature is Plato's *The Allegory of the Cave.* If you haven't read it, I would highly suggest it! The allegory tells of prisoners who have been chained up inside a cave their whole lives, never able to experience anything but the images of the shadows on the wall. This is their reality. This is all they have ever known. None of them can see anything but what is in front of them. They remain fixed in the same position, trapped in a cage of a false idea of what is real. Eventually, one is released from the chains and then the cave. The sight of the sun staggers the freed prisoner. He realizes everything he did not see. His concept of reality is expanded. He sees the sun and all which the sun illuminates. It is a new life for him because of what he can see.

You can have a similarly enlightening experience when you take a step back and look at where you are and where you want to be. It allows you to take an inventory of yourself. Not just an inventory of what you have done but what you are becoming (I'll talk about a "Be" bucket list in a later chapter).

I have met many people who have done this. They have taken off for six months or a year. They have quit their "real jobs" to find their calling. They search their heart and seek for who they really are. One man I know and admire, Steve Hargadon, was very successful in his position at his steady job in the Bay Area, California, but just didn't feel right. He quit his job and very quickly began to do consulting in education reform and educational technology. He is now one of the authorities in this field with one of the most visited blogs on the internet about edu-tech. I met a Franciscan monk in Jerusalem, Father Angelo, who was an extremely successful businessman in New York City for the first half of his life. One day, he felt very strongly that he was to give up money and live the life of a monk. He just felt like it was his calling. He gave up all his money and now lives as a spiritual guide to Christian pilgrims from around the world. He is one of the most amazing people I have ever met. Andrea Bocelli was once a defense attorney. Harrison Ford was once a carpenter. Sylvester Stallone once worked at a deli and a zoo (Huffington Post, 13 People Who Prove It's Never Too Late For A Career Change, June 24, 2013)

Walt Disney and J.K. Rowling were both fired from their desk jobs before they became some of the most well-known public figures of our time. Either these people had the courage to pause their daily routine, step outside themselves, and take a look, or they were forced to do so because they couldn't get their minds off of their true passion (Alana Horowitz, Business Insider, "15 People Who Were Fired Before They Became Filthy Rich" April 25, 2011.) When they stepped back, they found that what they were seeing was not what they wanted to become, and they got out of the cave.

It takes courage to step outside the comfort or security of our routine lives, but ask any of the people who have made the change, and they will tell you it is worth it. Find your patronus. Look for your "inner Rocky Balboa." Draw up your first draft of Mickey Mouse. I promise you, you'll be glad you did.

About the Author

Andrew Scot Proctor is the owner of TheReturnedMissionary.com, encouraging the tens of thousands of LDS missionaries who come home every year to continue to be productive, hardworking, faithful, and happy long after their full-time mission has ended. His goal with this blog is to help people know how they can live the gospel while living their dreams. He also owns the LDSMissionaries.com blog which has a following of over a half-million Facebook subscribers. *Live Your Mission: 21 Powerful Principles to Discover Your Life Mission after Your Mission* is the first book in the *Live My Gospel* book series. Subscribe to the email newsletter at TheReturnedMissionary.com to find out when the next book in the series is released.

Andy earned a bachelor of science in psychology from Brigham Young University and is moving forward in his career studying positive psychology and teaching people about the science of happiness and human flourishing. He has worked as a search engine optimizer at OrangeSoda.com and started his own small SEO business. He loves rollerblading on the boardwalk of any beach, long-exposure time-lapse photography, road trips with his wife Stacie, and doing missionary work using social media. Find and connect with him on any social media account on his website: www.andrewscotproctor.com.

Made in the USA
Charleston, SC
09 December 2015